CONTENTS

QUICK BREADS

HOWARD EARLY AND GLENDA MORRIS

THE CROSSING PRESS SPECIALTY COOKBOOKS

THE CROSSING PRESS **FREEDOM, CALIFORNIA**

Copyright © 1998 by Howard Early and Glenda Morris
Cover design by Victoria May
Cover photograph by Juliette Conroy
Interior design by Sheryl Karas
Printed in the U.S.A.

This book is dedicated to our students, who helped us learn during our seven years of teaching bread baking at The Baltimore School. More than that, the book is dedicated to the idea that bread baking is fun.

For information on bulk purchases or group discounts for this and other Crossing Press titles, please contact our Special Sales Manager at 800-777-1048 x214.

Visit our Web site on the Internet: www.crossingpress.com

Library of Congress Cataloging-in-Publication Data

Early, Howard.
    Quick breads / Howard Early and Glenda Morris.
        p. cm. -- (The Crossing Press specialty cookbooks)
    Rev. ed. of: Fast Breads! c1986.
    ISBN 0-89594-941-5
    1. Bread. 2. Quick and easy cookery. I. Morris, Glenda.
  II. Early, Howard. Fast Breads! III. Title IV. Series: Specialty cookbook series.
  TX769.E2   1998
  641.8'15--dc21   98-10591
                                                     CIP

INTRODUCTION

This is a book about making quick breads. Quick breads do not require a period of kneading or rising. Generally they go straight from the mixing bowl to the oven in a bread pan, muffin tin, or tin can. Quick breads are quick. As you become comfortable with your baking, you will have your quick bread oven-ready in ten to fifteen minutes—even less if you do a bit of advance preparation.

You can bake all of the basics—white, rye, whole wheat. You can select breads that are coarse and grainy, or breads that are almost like cake. You can bake a quick bread with almost any fruit or vegetable, and you can bake with nuts and seeds. You can make quick breads in the style of many different cuisines—Finnish flat breads or Indian chappatis. Although we present many dessert and festive breads, most of our breads are dinner breads.

Techniques

In most of the recipes that follow, we prepare the wet and the dry ingredients in separate containers. The dry ingredients are most conveniently assembled in a large mixing bowl. The wet ingredients can go into a one-quart jar or small bowl. Putting the liquids in a covered jar enables you to mix them by vigorously shaking the jar.

The chemistry of quick breads is such that no reaction occurs until the dry ingredients are moistened. So if you have time the night before or early in the morning, mix up the separate sets of ingredients. Then, when you are ready to bake, all you have to do is pour the wet ingredients into the bowl of dry ingredients, stir gently, spoon the batter into a well-greased bread pan, and bake.

There are a few breads in which you cut the butter into the dry ingredients. Those breads can't sit very long and should be baked soon after mixing.

When mixing the batter, stir quickly, but gently. Do not try to make the batter smooth; it should be coarse, but it shouldn't have big lumps. You also want to get the batter into the oven as quickly as you can (exceptions are noted). The reason for this is that as soon as you moisten the baking powder or soda, it begins to release carbon dioxide. You want that gas to be trapped in the batter to allow the bread to rise. Stir too long and too hard and much of the carbon dioxide will escape, leaving a flat, tough bread.

Bread Pans

Throughout the book we talk of small, medium-size, and large loaf pans. Large bread pans generally measure 9 inches by 5 inches. The medium-size pans are 1/2 to 1 inch smaller, usually 8 1/2 inches by 4 inches. Though that may seem like a small difference, the medium-size pan holds half a pound less of batter. Small pans hold about half as much as a large pan. They generally measure 7 1/2 inches by 3 inches.

Flour

Any flour you find in the supermarket is fine for making quick breads. We bake with unbleached white flour. You can use all-purpose white flour just as well.

In a fruit bread or subtly spiced bread, the whole wheat flavor may overpower your featured ingredients. Secondly, some adjustment in the recipe may be called for because the whole wheat flour will absorb more liquid than white flour. Use slightly less flour—about one quarter to one half cup less flour for most of the recipes in this book should be about right. Finally, a bread made entirely with whole wheat flour will be much denser. You will usually get a smaller, heavier, chewier loaf. For that reason we often combine unbleached and whole wheat flours.

In selecting the type of whole wheat flour, we find that soft wheat, usually identified as pastry flour, works better than the winter or hard wheat flour used in making yeast breads.

Whole wheat flour should be stored in a cool place and kept less than three months. Because this flour contains all of the kernel (including the wheat germ), it tends to become rancid more quickly than white flour.

Rising Agents

Baking powder and baking soda are the main leavening agents in quick breads. They both cause the bread to rise; however, they work slightly differently. All rising agents produce bubbles of carbon dioxide. The oven heat makes the bubbles expand rapidly so the dough rises. As the temperature of the dough increases to the temperature of the oven, the protein in the flour (and the milk and eggs) becomes rigid. The protein forms a solid cellular structure around the gas bubbles, creating the tiny holes that make the bread light.

Baking powder is usually a combination of one part baking soda (an alkali) and two parts of some finely powdered acid (calcium acid phosphate is among the more common). Usually cornstarch or rice flour is added to keep the mixture dry and to slow its reaction to the liquid. The baking powder will begin its rising action slowly when moistened, but its main rising action occurs when heated. This is why most of the powders on the market today are labeled "double-acting."

In breads where the liquid ingredients are highly acid, for example, buttermilk, sour cream, or orange juice, you can use just baking soda for leavening. Since the chemical interaction in these breads may be slower, the batters can be gently kneaded (as in Irish Soda Bread or some scones). Kneading helps develop the protein network that will trap the escaping gas. Since you cannot control the acid level of the liquids you use, breads relying solely on baking soda may be more variable.

Cooking Oil, Shortening, Butter, and Margarine

You can't bake without some sort of oil or fat and get good breads. (There are, as one might expect, a few exceptions to this rule.) The cooking oil or fat will do four things for the bread: increase the volume, soften the texture, add to the flavor, and help in maintaining freshness.

The various fats do work differently. An animal shortening, such as butter, contributes greatly to flavor and texture. A plant oil, such as sunflower oil, is tasteless, but it does make for a soft bread and coarse crumb.

Don't worry about what you use. Use what you have on hand or find convenient or economical, without falling into a rigid pattern. Vary the oils when you can and you will find that you like some better than others. For example, we find that Irish Soda Bread is particularly delicious with butter and, because of the way it is made, it does demand a semi-solid shortening.

A word about "cutting in the butter." If that is what the recipe calls for, do it. Use ice cold butter. Cut it into small chunks, say about the size of a half teaspoon or smaller, and add the chunks directly to the flour. Then using two knives, or a fork, or your fingertips, break up the chunks so that they are fully incorporated into the flour. You could also use a food processor, pulsing carefully. The flour will then look like cornmeal—it will appear grainy and yellow. Why bother? Well, what happens is that the butter melts during the baking procedure, creating a light, flaky texture. Make the same recipe with a liquid oil and the bread will be much denser.

Sweetening Agents

Some sweeteners are fairly strong and distinctive. Molasses is a good example. Some sweeteners seem to blend better with some flours. Honey and whole wheat or maple sugar and oat are examples of fine blends. We found that in rye and some oat breads, malted barley syrup is an excellent sweetener. It can be used in the same amounts as white sugar and it imparts a gentle taste. Look for malted barley syrup in natural food stores.

Baking Times

The baking times we give are as accurate as we can make them. However, there are so many factors that influence baking times—including the accuracy of the thermostat in your oven, the humidity, and altitude—that our time estimates may have to be reduced by as much as ten minutes. If you have doubts, check the bread every five minutes or so when it is close to getting done.

All of these recipes have been established without preheating the oven. Most stoves move up to their temperature pretty quickly. Besides an oven that is initially too high may cause the bread to set before it has fully risen.

When is the bread done? Look at the bread, thump it, poke it, listen to it, and smell it. When your kitchen fills with the wonderful smell of baking bread, you know it is getting close to being done.

Removing the Bread From the Pan

Some breads can be served right out of the oven, but others, especially those that are heavy in fruit or crumbly in texture, should cool first. Place the bread pan on a rack where air can circulate around all sides. Give the bread almost ten minutes to cool and contract. It should then come out of the pan quite easily. Leaving it in the pan longer can be a disaster; the crust becomes soggy from the condensation of the pan.

Eat and Enjoy

Lest you become overwhelmed by all of our bits of advice, remember that bread baking is enjoyable. While there are a few people who were weaned on supermarket white bread and cannot eat anything else, most people are genuinely excited by home-baked bread. At potluck dinners, the home-baked bread usually disappears first.

As a beginning bread baker, you might consider inviting a friend to join you in some of your first ventures. It is a great way to socialize, and we have found that two cooks don't spoil the bread.

BASIC SEMI-SWEET WHITE BREAD

This is as simple as a quick bread can be. It is rich and cakelike, but not too sweet.

Dry Ingredients

2 cups unbleached flour
½ cup sugar
2 teaspoons baking powder
½ teaspoon salt

Wet Ingredients

1 cup milk
1 egg, beaten
2 tablespoons oil

Mix together the dry ingredients.

Stir together the wet ingredients. Combine the wet and dry ingredients very lightly. The batter will be very runny.

Pour into a greased medium-size loaf pan and bake at 350° F. for 40 minutes. Let the bread cool for 10 minutes before removing it from the pan. Cut into thick slices while still warm and serve with sweet butter.

CARAWAY WHITE BREAD

The texture of this bread is rough, and the high density of caraway seeds gives it a unique flavor and chewy texture. Caraway seeds are an aid to digestion.

Dry Ingredients

1½ cups unbleached flour
1 tablespoon sugar
1 tablespoon caraway seeds
¼ teaspoon salt
2 teaspoons baking powder

Wet Ingredients

⅓ cup chilled butter
1 egg, beaten
½ cup milk

Combine the dry ingredients.

Cut the butter into the dry ingredients with a pastry cutter or work it in with your fingers until the mixture resembles a coarse meal. Mix together the egg and milk.

Lightly mix together the wet and dry ingredients.

Spread the batter into a greased flat pan. An 11½-inch by 5½-inch casserole dish is ideal.

Bake at 350° F. for 30 minutes. Serve warm, directly from the pan.

This makes an easily sliced, attractive flat loaf that's about 2 inches high.

IRISH SODA BREAD

Dry Ingredients

2 cups unbleached flour
¾ teaspoon baking soda
½ teaspoon baking powder
1 tablespoon sugar
¼ teaspoon salt

Wet Ingredients

6 tablespoons chilled butter
½ cup buttermilk or more as needed

Optional

¼ cup dried currants or ½ cup raisins and
  a pinch of cardamom added with the
  buttermilk

Mix together the dry ingredients. Cut the butter into the dry ingredients with a pastry cutter or work it in with your fingers until the mixture resembles a coarse meal.

Pour in the buttermilk and mix gently. The batter should be moist. If it is too dry, add up to 3 more tablespoons buttermilk. The dough should be firm, not crumbly. Knead the dough briefly and gently on a lightly floured board. Shape into a ground loaf. Brush the top of the loaf with buttermilk, and cut a cross on the top. This keeps the bread from developing random cracks on the surface.

Bake on a greased baking sheet or skillet at 375° F. for 40 to 45 minutes. Serve directly from the oven.

GARLIC WHITE BREAD

This is a delightfully pungent bread, and you can vary the filling according to your taste and sense of adventure. Eat it warm.

Dry Ingredients

3 cups unbleached flour
1 tablespoon baking powder
½ teaspoon salt

Wet Ingredients

1 egg, beaten
¾ cup milk

Filling Ingredients

6 tablespoons softened butter
3 or more garlic cloves, crushed
2 teaspoons chopped parsley (dried or fresh)
⅛ teaspoon white pepper
¼ teaspoon paprika

Mix together the dry ingredients.

Mix together the wet ingredients.

Mix the wet and dry ingredients together. Turn the dough onto a floured surface. Knead gently a few times. Roll it out (or flatten with your hands) to a rectangle that is about 10 inches by 12 inches.

Mix together the filling ingredients. Sprinkle the filling over the dough. Roll up tightly as you would a jelly roll. Tuck the ends under and place in a large greased bread pan.

Bake at 350° F. for about 45 minutes.

Let the bread cool for 10 minutes before removing it from the pan.

BASIC WHOLE WHEAT BREAD

This bread is our straightforward adaptation of the traditional Irish soda bread.

Dry Ingredients

2 cups whole wheat flour
¾ teaspoon baking soda
½ teaspoon baking powder
½ teaspoon salt

Wet Ingredients

6 tablespoons chilled butter
1 cup buttermilk
1 tablespoon honey

Combine the dry ingredients.

Cut the butter into the dry ingredients with a pastry cutter or work it in with your fingers until the mixture resembles coarse meal.

Mix together the buttermilk and honey. Mix into the dry ingredients.

Knead the dough briefly and gently.

Place in a greased medium-size bread pan or shape into a round loaf and place in a greased pie tin. Bake at 350° F. for 40 to 50 minutes.

Let the bread cool for 10 minutes before removing it from the pan.

WHEAT AND SOY BREAD

Soy flour is milled from soybeans. Rich in protein, soy flour combined with whole wheat gives a high-quality protein bread. Soy flour is also rich in minerals and B vitamins so this bread is supernutritious. The soy adds a full-bodied taste to the bread.

Dry Ingredients

2 cups whole wheat flour
½ cup soy flour
2 teaspoons baking powder
½ teaspoon cinnamon
¼ teaspoon salt

Wet Ingredients

¾ cup milk
2 eggs, beaten
¼ cup oil
¼ cup molasses
½ cup raisins
Grated rind of 1 orange

Mix together the dry ingredients.

Stir together the milk, eggs, oil, and molasses. Add the raisins and orange rind.

Combine the dry and wet ingredients lightly.

Spoon into a small greased loaf pan or spoon into miniature greased loaf pans to make an unusual dinner roll. Bake at 375° F. for 45 minutes. For the miniature loaves, reduce the baking time to 25 minutes.

Let the bread cool for 10 minutes before removing it from the pan.

WHEAT-BRAN-SOY BREAD

This is a fine, simple dinner bread that is great served piping hot from the oven.

Dry Ingredients

2 cups whole wheat flour
½ cup soy flour
¼ cup wheat bran
1 teaspoon baking soda
½ teaspoon salt

Wet Ingredients

1½ cups buttermilk
¼ cup honey
2 tablespoons oil

Mix together the dry ingredients.

Combine the wet ingredients.

Mix the dry and wet ingredients together. Pour into a well-greased medium-size loaf pan.

Bake at 325° F. for about 1 hour.

Let the bread cool for 10 minutes before removing it from the pan.

WHEAT GERM HONEY BREAD

*Proteins, iron, vitamin E, and B vitamins—that's
what you get with this honey-flavored loaf. Using
different kinds of honey changes the taste of this loaf
considerably. For example, the strong taste of buckwheat honey makes this more like a molasses bread,
while the mild taste of most supermarket brands
merely adds the suggestion of a honey taste.*

Dry Ingredients
1½ cups whole wheat flour
1 cup wheat germ
2 teaspoons baking powder
¼ teaspoon baking soda
¼ teaspoon salt

Wet Ingredients
¾ cup milk
¼ cup oil
¼ cup honey
1 egg, beaten

Mix together the dry ingredients.

Mix together the wet ingredients.

Combine the wet and dry ingredients
lightly.

Pour the batter into a small greased loaf
pan. Bake at 350° F. for 30 minutes.

Let the bread cool for 10 minutes before
removing it from the pan.

GLENDA'S PROTEIN BREAD

Glenda developed this to counter the image of dry, heavy, tasteless "health" breads. This is sweet, moist, fruity, and crunchy. It is especially high in protein.

Dry Ingredients

2 cups whole wheat flour
1½ cups unbleached flour
⅔ cup nonfat dry milk
⅓ cup wheat germ
2 teaspoons baking powder
½ teaspoon baking soda
½ teaspoon salt

Wet Ingredients

¾ cup orange juice
3 eggs
½ cup oil or softened butter
¼ cup light molasses
¼ cup honey
1 medium-size banana
½ cup raisins
⅓ cup chopped dried apricots
½ cup chopped dates

Mix together the dry ingredients.

Combine the orange juice, eggs, oil or butter, molasses, honey, and banana in a blender. Blend until smooth. Add the raisins, apricots, and dates.

Combine the liquid-plus-fruit and dry ingredients lightly.

Spoon into a large greased loaf pan.

Bake at 325° F. for 60 to 70 minutes.

Let the bread cool for 10 minutes before removing it from the pan. This is a heavy bread and should be removed very gently.

Baked Boston Brown Bread

This is a somewhat unconventional Boston brown bread in that it is baked, not steamed.

Dry Ingredients

2 cups whole wheat or graham flour
½ cup cornmeal
3 tablespoons soy flour
2 teaspoons baking soda
½ teaspoon salt
1 cup raisins

Wet Ingredients

¼ cup molasses
1 cup buttermilk

Mix together the dry ingredients.

Mix together the wet ingredients.

Mix together the wet and dry ingredients.

Pour into a greased medium-size loaf pan. Let stand for 30 minutes.

Bake at 350° F. for 40 to 50 minutes.

Let the bread cool for 10 minutes before removing it from the pan.

COFFEE OAT BREAD

This bread is not very sweet, and the coffee imparts a distinctive taste. For an even stronger coffee flavor, espresso can be substituted in full or in part for the coffee. Serve this bread with softened cream cheese.

Dry Ingredients

1½ cups oat flour
1½ cups unbleached flour
⅓ cup sugar
½ cup nonfat dry milk
¼ teaspoon salt
½ teaspoon cinnamon
1½ teaspoons baking powder

Wet Ingredients

2 tablespoons softened butter
1½ cups cold strong coffee
1 egg
1 teaspoon vanilla extract

Combine the dry ingredients in a mixing bowl.

Combine the butter, coffee, egg, and vanilla extract in a blender at a moderate speed until well blended.

Stir together the wet and dry ingredients. Spoon into a greased medium-size loaf pan.

Bake at 350° F. for 50 to 60 minutes.

Let the bread cool for 10 minutes before removing it from the pan.

OATMEAL FRUIT BREAD

Use a combination of your favorite dried fruits for this bread—and don't forget the raisins. We like to include a little of everything: pears, peaches, nectarines, apricots, prunes, apples, and golden raisins. Cut the fruit into small pieces.

Dry Ingredients

2 cups unbleached flour
1½ cups oat flour
¼ cup sugar
¼ teaspoon salt
2 teaspoons baking powder
½ teaspoon baking soda

Wet Ingredients

½ cup orange juice
½ cup pineapple juice
¼ cup orange marmalade (or pineapple preserves)
1 egg, beaten
1 tablespoon oil
1 cup chopped dried fruit

Mix together the dry ingredients.

Stir together the orange juice, pineapple juice, marmalade, egg, and oil. Add the dried fruit.

Combine the liquid-plus-fruit and dry ingredients.

Pour into a greased medium-size loaf pan. Bake at 350° F. for 50 to 60 minutes.

Let the bread cool for 10 minutes before removing it from the pan.

HOWARD'S MAPLE OAT BREAD

Howard has been experimenting with maple syrup and maple sugar for years. This was his first successful maple bread. It's a firm, chewy bread with the clear taste of maple. Be sure to use 100 percent maple syrup; pancake syrup just doesn't have enough maple taste to be used here.

Dry Ingredients

2 cups unbleached flour
1 cup oat flour
2 teaspoons baking powder
¼ cup maple sugar

Wet Ingredients

1½ cups milk
1 egg, beaten
1 tablespoon oil
½ cup pure maple syrup
½ cup golden raisins

Mix together the dry ingredients.

Mix together the milk, egg, oil, and maple syrup. Add the raisins.

Combine the wet and dry ingredients. Spoon into a greased medium-size loaf pan. Let it sit for 10 to 15 minutes before baking.

Bake at 350° F. for 35 to 40 minutes.

Let the bread cool for 10 minutes before removing it from the pan.

HEAVY/LIGHT OAT BREAD

Dry Ingredients

1 cup whole wheat flour
1 cup oat flour
½ teaspoon salt
1 teaspoon baking soda
1 teaspoon cinnamon
½ cup dark raisins

Wet Ingredients

¼ cup honey
1 cup buttermilk
3 tablespoons melted shortening or oil
1½ teaspoons vanilla extract

Combine the dry ingredients. Mix together the wet ingredients. Pour the wet ingredients into the dry and combine just until moistened. Spoon the batter into a greased 7-cup mold (for a steamed bread) or a medium-size bread pan (for a baked bread).

To steam the bread, cover the mold with a double thickness of waxed paper or aluminum foil and tie it on securely. Place on a trivet in a deep pot. Add enough boiling water to come halfway up the sides of the mold. Cover the pot and steam for 1½ hours. Serve the bread the next day.

To bake the bread, bake at 350° F. for about 1 hour. Let the bread cool for 10 minutes before removing it from the pan. Serve this bread warm.

DILL AND CARAWAY OAT BREAD

This is a modest dinner bread with a pronounced flavor of dill and caraway.

Dry Ingredients

1 cup oat flour
2 cups unbleached flour
½ cup nonfat dry milk
¼ teaspoon salt
2 teaspoons caraway seeds
1 teaspoon dill seeds
2 teaspoons baking powder

Wet Ingredients

1 cup water
1½ tablespoons oil
2 teaspoons malted barley syrup
  (brown sugar may be substituted)
1 egg, beaten

Combine all the ingredients and spoon into a greased medium-size loaf pan.

Bake at 350° F. for 40 to 50 minutes.

Let the bread cool for 10 minutes before removing it from the pan.

Basic Rye Bread

Dry Ingredients

1 cup rye flour
1 cup unbleached flour
1 tablespoon sugar
¾ teaspoon baking soda
½ teaspoon baking powder
½ teaspoon salt
1 tablespoon caraway seeds

Wet Ingredients

6 tablespoons chilled butter
¾ cup milk
⅓ cup golden raisins (optional)

Mix together the dry ingredients.

Cut the butter into the dry ingredients with a pastry cutter or work it in with your fingers until it resembles coarse meal.

Mix in the milk and raisins.

Stir quickly, then spoon into a greased medium-size loaf pan. Bake at 375° F. for 45 minutes.

Let the bread cool for 10 minutes before removing it from the pan.

Dark Rye Bread

This is our quick bread version of a traditional old world black bread. The addition of vinegar gives it a light sourdough taste.

Dry Ingredients

1½ cups rye flour
2½ cups unbleached flour
2 teaspoons baking powder
½ teaspoon salt
½ teaspoon baking soda
1 tablespoon caraway seeds
¼ teaspoon crushed fennel seeds

Wet Ingredients

1 cup buttermilk
½ cup milk
⅜ cup cold strong coffee
¼ cup oil
3 tablespoons light molasses
½ ounce unsweetened chocolate, melted
1 tablespoon cider or white vinegar

Combine the dry and wet ingredients. This makes a thick, heavy batter. Spoon it into large greased loaf pan and let it sit for 15 to 20 minutes.

Bake at 350° F. for 45 to 50 minutes.

Let the bread cool for 10 minutes before removing it from the pan.

Potato Rye Bread

Add potatoes to bread and you get a moister and lighter bread. To prepare the potato for the bread, peel and shred 1 small potato. Cook it in 1 1/2 to 2 cups water (enough to cover the potato shreds fully) for about 10 minutes.

Dry Ingredients

1 ¾ cups rye flour
¾ cup unbleached flour
3 tablespoons nonfat dry milk
1 teaspoon baking powder
1 tablespoon caraway seeds
½ teaspoon salt

Wet Ingredients

½ cup drained cooked shredded potato
½ cup potato cooking water (reserve the rest to be used in soup or keep in the refrigerator for other breads)
2 tablespoons oil
2 tablespoons malted barley syrup or light molasses
1 tablespoon grated orange peel

Combine all the ingredients. The batter will be very heavy. Place in a small greased loaf pan and let it sit for 15 to 20 minutes.

Bake at 350° F. for 45 minutes.

Let the bread cool for 10 minutes before removing it from the pan.

TRITICALE BREAD

Triticale (pronounced trit-i-kay-lee) is a newly popular grain that is a cross between wheat and rye. It is very nutritious and, because the taste is mild, it is often liked by people who ordinarily don't like whole wheat. The cinnamon in this bread is very subtle and will be a nice mystery ingredient to most tasters.

Dry Ingredients

2 ½ cups triticale flour
½ teaspoon cinnamon
¼ teaspoon salt
1 teaspoon baking soda

Wet Ingredients

1 egg, beaten
¼ cup molasses (or malted barley syrup)
¼ cup oil
Grated rind from 1 lemon
⅔ cup yogurt or sour cream

Mix together the dry ingredients.

Combine the wet ingredients.

Mix together the wet and dry ingredients. The batter will be quite heavy. Spoon into a greased medium-size loaf pan.

Bake at 375° F. for about 45 minutes.

Let the bread cool for 10 minutes before removing it from the pan.

BASIC BRAN BREAD

Dry Ingredients

2 cups wheat bran
1 cup unbleached flour
1½ teaspoons baking powder
¾ teaspoon baking soda
½ teaspoon salt

Wet Ingredients

1¼ cups buttermilk
1 egg, beaten
¼ cup honey

Combine all the ingredients. Pour into a small greased loaf pan.

Bake at 375° F. for 1 hour.

Let the bread cool for 10 minutes before removing it from the pan.

BRAN FIG BREAD

Dry Ingredients

1½ cups wheat bran
1½ cups unbleached flour
1½ teaspoons baking powder
¼ teaspoon salt

Wet Ingredients

1½ cups milk
½ cup dark brown sugar
¼ cup oil
¾ cup chopped figs

Mix together the dry ingredients.

Combine the wet ingredients.

Combine the dry and wet ingredients. Spoon into a greased medium-size loaf pan.

Bake at 375° F. for 60 to 70 minutes.

Let the bread cool for 10 minutes before removing it from the pan.

Raisin Bran Bread

This heavy, sweet brown bread is complemented by mounds of cream cheese.

Wet Ingredients

1 cup raisins (dark or golden or a combination)
1½ cups warm water
1 egg, beaten
2 tablespoons oil
½ teaspoon vanilla extract

Dry Ingredients

1 cup wheat bran
1¾ cups unbleached flour
¾ cup light brown sugar
2 teaspoons baking powder
½ teaspoon baking soda

To plump the raisins, combine the raisins and water. Let stand for 30 minutes. Add the eggs and vanilla.

Combine the dry ingredients.

Combine the wet and dry ingredients lightly. Spoon the batter into a well-buttered 1-pound coffee can or several smaller cans. (The cans should be about two-thirds full.)

Bake at 350° F. for 50 to 60 minutes.

Let the bread cool for 10 minutes before removing it from the can. Allow the flavors to blend overnight before serving. This bread keeps well.

DATE BRAN BREAD

This is an excellent fruit bread with a coarse texture. It is best served cold.

Wet Ingredients

1 cup chopped dates
1 cup boiling water
1 egg
¼ cup honey
½ teaspoon vanilla extract

Dry Ingredients

¾ cup whole wheat flour
¾ cup unbleached flour
1 cup wheat bran
⅓ cup wheat germ
1 teaspoon baking powder
½ teaspoon baking soda
½ teaspoon salt
½ cup chopped nuts (optional)

Combine the dates and boiling water. Set aside to cool.

Beat together the egg, honey, and vanilla. Add to the cooled date mixture.

Combine the dry ingredients.

Combine the wet and dry ingredients lightly. Spoon into a small greased loaf pan.

Bake at 350° F. for 1 hour.

Let the bread cool for 10 minutes before removing it from the pan.

TBS Light Buckwheat Bread

TBS was the acronym of The Baltimore School where we taught and experimented with bread baking for seven oven-filled years. Howard developed this bread for all of those who love buckwheat pancakes. Even if you don't normally care for buckwheat, you will find this a wholesomely tasty bread.

Dry Ingredients

1 cup light buckwheat flour
1½ cups unbleached flour
¼ cup sugar
1½ teaspoons baking powder
1 teaspoon baking soda
¼ teaspoon salt

Wet Ingredients

1 cup milk
1 egg, beaten
2 tablespoons oil

Mix together the dry ingredients.

Mix together the wet ingredients.

Pour the wet ingredients into the dry and mix together lightly. Spoon into a greased medium-size loaf pan.

Bake at 350° F. for 40 to 45 minutes.

Let the bread cool for 10 minutes before removing it from the pan.

JEANNE'S RICE BREAD

The texture of this bread is like corn bread—except for the crunchy crust. For variety and moistness, add 1 1/2 medium bananas, mashed, and reduce the milk to 1/2 cup.

Dry Ingredients

2¾ cups cream of rice (one 16-ounce package)
3 tablespoons sugar
¼ teaspoon salt
2 teaspoons baking powder

Wet Ingredients

1 cup milk
1 egg, beaten
3 tablespoons oil

Combine the dry ingredients.

Mix together the wet ingredients.

Combine the dry and wet ingredients. Pour into small greased cans (holding 1 to ½ cups) or a small greased loaf pan. Fill close to the top since this bread will not rise very much.

Bake at 350° F. for about 45 minutes. Reduce the time by 5 to 10 minutes for the small pans.

Let the bread cool for 10 minutes before removing it from the pan.

BUCKWHEAT GROATS BREAD

Now if you really want the full taste of buckwheat, this bread is it. It is very strong tasting, so we just make a small loaf.

Wet Ingredients

¼ **cup buckwheat groats**
½ **cup water**
6 **tablespoons butter**
¾ **cup milk**
2 **tablespoons dark brown sugar**

Dry Ingredients

1¾ **cups unbleached flour**
1 **teaspoon baking soda**
½ **teaspoon baking powder**

First, prepare the groats. Combine the groats and water in the top of a double boiler and cook for about 30 minutes, or until all the water is absorbed (or follow the directions on the package).

While the groats are still warm, add the butter. Stir until the butter is melted and absorbed. Then add the milk and sugar.

Mix together the dry ingredients.

Combine the groats mixture with the dry ingredients.

Spoon the batter into a small greased loaf pan. Bake at 375° F. for 40 to 45 minutes.

Let the bread cool for 10 minutes before removing it from the pan.

New England Corn Bread

While corn breads have been associated with Southern cookery, this variation, which relies on maple syrup, has no regional bounds.

Dry Ingredients

1 cup cornmeal
1 cup unbleached flour
2 teaspoons cream of tartar
1 teaspoon baking soda
½ teaspoon salt

Wet Ingredients

1 cup milk
1 egg
¼ cup melted butter
¼ cup pure maple syrup

Mix together the dry ingredients.

Combine the wet ingredients in a blender and process until smooth.

Combine the dry and wet ingredients, mixing gently but well. Spoon into a flat buttered 8-inch or 9-inch square baking pan.

Bake at 400° F. for 25 to 30 minutes.

Serve warm, directly from the pan. Or let cool for 5 to 10 minutes, then remove from the pan.

SOUTHWESTERN CORN BREAD

Add some jalapeño peppers, cheese, and onion and you produce another regional variation. This is a genuinely zesty bread. It makes a tasty accompaniment to soup.

Dry Ingredients

1¼ cups cornmeal
½ cup unbleached flour
½ teaspoon salt
2 teaspoons baking powder
¼ cup nonfat dry milk

Wet Ingredients

2 eggs, beaten
¾ cup water
¼ cup oil
3 or 4 chopped jalapeño peppers
1 cup shredded sharp cheddar cheese
½ medium-size onion, grated

Mix together the dry ingredients.

Combine the eggs, water, and oil. Beat well. Add to the dry ingredients. Then mix in jalapeños, cheese, and onion. Pour into a lightly greased 8-inch or 9-inch baking pan.

Bake at 425° F. for about 30 minutes.

Serve warm, directly from the baking pan. Or let cool for 10 minutes, then remove it from the pan.

Coconut Corn Bread

You can add a substantial number of ingredients to basic corn bread. As long as you adjust the wet ingredients so your batter isn't too runny, you can pretty much count on a successful outcome. In this basic recipe, we substituted coconut milk for plain milk and then added shredded coconut to enhance the flavor and texture. This is a good time to extend the "white theme" by using white cornmeal.

Dry Ingredients

1 cup unbleached flour
¾ cup cornmeal
1 tablespoon baking powder
½ teaspoon salt

Wet Ingredients

1 cup coconut milk
½ cup oil
1 egg, beaten
⅓ cup shredded sweetened coconut
  (if you use unsweetened coconut, add 3 tablespoons sugar)

Mix together the dry ingredients.

Mix together the wet ingredients.

Combine the dry and wet ingredients. Spoon into a buttered 8-inch or 9-inch baking pan.

Bake at 400° F. for 25 to 30 minutes.

Serve warm, directly from the pan. Or let cool for 5 to 10 minutes, then remove from the pan.

SOUR CREAM CORN BREAD

We don't know who first substituted sour cream for milk or water, but it was a brilliant stroke in the art of baking. The sour cream changes the texture of the bread. The graininess is almost gone, but the thick crumb of corn bread remains—as does its sweetness.

Dry Ingredients

1 cup cornmeal
¾ cup unbleached flour
3 tablespoons sugar
1 ½ teaspoons cream of tartar
1 teaspoon baking soda
½ teaspoon salt

Wet Ingredients

1 cup sour cream
¼ cup milk
1 egg
2 tablespoons oil

Mix together the dry ingredients.

Beat together the wet ingredients.

Combine the dry and wet ingredients. Spoon into a well-buttered 8-inch or 9-inch baking pan.

Bake for 10 minutes at 375° F.; then reduce the heat to 350° F. and bake for 15 minutes more.

Serve warm, directly from the baking pan. Or let cool for 10 minutes, then remove it from the pan.

PEANUT RYE BREAD

This bread yields a good peanutty taste—not of peanut butter, but of peanuts. It has a very rough texture and a good, chewy quality.

Dry Ingredients

1 cup roasted unsalted peanuts
1 cup rye flour
2 tablespoons light brown sugar
1 ½ teaspoons grated orange peel
½ teaspoon salt
2 teaspoons baking powder

Wet Ingredients

¾ cup milk
3 tablespoons oil
⅓ cup golden raisins

Start with 1 cup roasted, unsalted peanuts and grind them in a blender or food processor until you have a coarse meal. Measure out ¾ cup peanut flour. Combine with the remaining dry ingredients.

Mix together the wet ingredients.

Combine the dry and wet ingredients and mix just until blended.

Place in a small greased loaf pan. Bake at 350° F. for 40 to 45 minutes.

Let the bread cool for 10 to 15 minutes before removing it from the pan.

Poppy Seed Bread

This bread is crust to crust seeds with just enough dough to hold them together. If you really love the taste and crunch of poppy seeds, use the 3/4 cup of seeds called for in this recipe. If you are fainthearted, use only about 1/2 cup seeds.

Dry Ingredients

2 cups unbleached flour
¼ cup brown rice flour
2 teaspoons baking powder
¼ teaspoon salt
¾ cup poppy seeds

Wet Ingredients

½ cup softened butter
½ cup sugar
1 egg
1 teaspoon vanilla extract
Grated rind of ½ lemon
1¼ cups milk

Combine the dry ingredients.

Cream together the butter and sugar. Add the egg, vanilla, lemon rind, and milk. Mix well.

Mix together the wet and dry ingredients until just blended. Spoon into a small well-greased baking pan, roughly 6 by 12 inches.

Bake at 350° F. for 45 to 50 minutes.

Serve warm, directly from the pan. The bread will be about 1 inch high. Serve it in thin slices.

WHOLE GRAIN POPPY SEED BREAD

Glenda developed this poppy seed dinner bread. It is an even-grained, nutritious, and tasty bread with plenty of poppy seed crunch. Experiment with the amount of seeds you add until it suits your taste. Serve it warm for dinner.

Do buy poppy seeds in bulk as they are outrageously expensive if purchased in grocery store tins.

Dry Ingredients

1¾ cups whole wheat flour
¼ cup brown rice flour
½ cup poppy seeds
½ teaspoon baking soda
1½ teaspoons baking powder
½ teaspoon salt

Wet Ingredients

¼ cup softened butter
1 egg, beaten
1 cup yogurt
3 tablespoons honey
1 teaspoon vanilla extract

Combine the dry ingredients.

Mix together the wet ingredients.

Mix together the wet and dry ingredients.

Pour into a small greased loaf pan.

Bake at 350° F. for about 50 minutes.

Let the bread cool for 5 to 10 minutes before removing it from the pan.

WHITE POPPY SEED BREAD

White poppy seeds are hard to find though they are used often in Indian and Middle Eastern confections. They are worth the hunt. White poppy seeds make an unusual bread. This recipe produces one small loaf of a somewhat crumbly, good-keeping, subtly nutty-tasting bread. Serve it any time.

Dry Ingredients

2 cups unbleached flour
½ cup brown rice flour
1 teaspoon baking powder
2 teaspoons baking soda
¼ teaspoon salt
⅓ cup white poppy seeds
½ cup sugar

Wet Ingredients

½ cup oil
¾ cup milk
1 egg, beaten
1 teaspoon vanilla extract

Mix together the dry ingredients.

Combine the wet ingredients.

Combine the dry and wet ingredients. Pour into a small greased loaf pan.

Bake at 350° F. for about 45 minutes.

Let the bread cool in the pan for 10 minutes. Be gentle in removing it from the pan since it is fragile.

SESAME SEED BREAD

Sesame seeds are native to India and are rich in vitamins, minerals, and protein. They are especially rich in calcium and lecithin. This bread is permeated by the wonderful nutty taste of sesame; it makes another good dinner bread.

Dry Ingredients

**2 cups whole wheat flour or 2½ cups
    unbleached flour**
⅓ cup sugar
2 teaspoons baking powder
½ cup sesame seeds
½ teaspoon salt

Wet Ingredients

¼ cup oil
2 eggs, beaten
⅔ cup milk

Combine the dry ingredients.

Beat together the wet ingredients.

Combine the wet and dry ingredients. Spoon the batter into a small greased loaf pan.

Bake at 350° F. for 40 to 50 minutes. Let the bread cool for 5 to 10 minutes before removing it from the pan. Serve warm or cold.

SESAME-MILLET BREAD

Sesame-millet is a very popular yeast bread in San Francisco. Glenda decided to experiment with making a quick bread after finding millet flour in a health food store. (Once again, you could make your own flour by pulverizing the seeds in a blender or food processor.) Millet is the seed of a type of grass plant. This is another bread that is best eaten warm.

Dry Ingredients

1 cup millet flour
1 cup whole wheat flour
¼ cup brown rice flour
½ cup roasted sesame seeds
2 teaspoons baking powder
½ teaspoon salt
¼ teaspoon baking soda

Wet Ingredients

3 tablespoons honey
1 egg
¼ cup oil
1 cup yogurt

Mix together the dry ingredients.

Beat together the wet ingredients.

Combine the wet and dry ingredients lightly. Spoon into a small greased loaf pan.

Bake at 350° F. for about 50 minutes.

Let the bread cool for 5 to 10 minutes before removing it from the pan.

Sunflower Rye Bread

We had never baked with sunflower seeds until we encountered Stella Standard's Our Daily Bread. We adapted this recipe from her interesting collection. It has a rich, crunchy taste and rough texture.

You can buy shelled sunflower seeds or sunflower meal in many health food stores; however, the meal usually comes in large cans. To ensure that the flavor and nutrition is at its best, grind your own.

Dry Ingredients

¾ cup sunflower meal
1 cup rye flour
¼ cup unbleached flour
2 teaspoons baking powder
3 tablespoons brown sugar
½ teaspoon cinnamon
½ teaspoon crushed anise
¼ teaspoon salt

Wet Ingredients

1 cup milk
3 tablespoons oil

Mix together the dry ingredients.

Mix together the wet ingredients.

Combine the dry and wet ingredients, mixing lightly. Spoon into a small greased loaf pan.

Bake at 350° F. for 35 minutes.

Let the bread cool for 10 minutes before removing it from the pan.

Peanut Butter Bread

The taste is surprisingly rich and buttery, especially considering the small amount of peanut butter used. The bread crumbles and does not keep well; but fresh out of the oven, it makes even the most exacting peanut butter lover happy.

Dry Ingredients

1 ¼ cups unbleached flour
¾ cup oat flour
2 tablespoons sugar
1 grated orange rind
½ teaspoon salt
2 teaspoons baking powder

Wet Ingredients

¼ cup smooth peanut butter
¼ cup oil
¾ cup milk

Mix together the dry ingredients.

Mix together the wet ingredients.

Combine the wet and dry ingredients lightly. Spoon into a small greased loaf pan.

Bake at 375° F. for 50 minutes.

Let the bread cool for 10 minutes before removing it from the pan. This is a very fragile bread and requires gentle treatment. It slices best with a sharp bread knife.

This is a great bread for brunch or snacks.

OLD-TIME PEANUT BUTTER BREAD

Old-time peanut butter, or the kind you grind your-self at the food co-op, is known for the way it sticks to the roof of your mouth. This bread comes close to that old-fashioned quality.

Dry Ingredients

2 cups unbleached flour
⅓ cup sugar
½ teaspoon salt
2 teaspoons baking powder

Wet Ingredients

1 cup peanut butter
1¼ cups milk
2 eggs

Mix together the dry ingredients. Mix in the peanut butter.

Beat together the milk and eggs.

Combine the wet and dry ingredients lightly. Spoon into a small greased loaf pan.

Bake at 350° F. for 50 to 60 minutes.

Let the bread cool for 10 minutes before removing it from the pan.

CHOCOLATE SPICE BREAD

This highly spiced bread is dark, dense, and delight-fully bitter. Serve it after it has cooled, so that the spices have a chance to blend and mellow. This can be a surprising accompaniment to curried dishes.

Dry Ingredients

2 cups unbleached flour
¼ cup sugar
½ teaspoon ginger
¼ teaspoon mace
¼ teaspoon nutmeg
¼ teaspoon cloves
¼ teaspoon cinnamon
1½ teaspoons baking soda

Wet Ingredients

¾ cup buttermilk
¼ cup light molasses
2 ounces unsweetened chocolate, melted

Combine the dry ingredients.

Mix together the wet ingredients.

Combine the wet and dry ingredients. Pour into a small greased loaf pan.

Bake at 325° F. for 30 minutes.

Let the bread cool for 10 minutes before removing it from the pan.

SOUR CREAM CHOCOLATE BREAD

Swirling the chocolate throughout produces a marbled appearance. This is a dessert bread that also goes well at breakfast with eggs. For dessert, it is an unusual accompaniment for fruit.

Dry Ingredients

2 ¼ cups unbleached flour
1 teaspoon baking powder
½ teaspoon baking soda
½ teaspoon salt

Wet Ingredients

½ cup sugar
2 eggs
1 cup sour cream
6 tablespoons grated semi-sweet
  chocolate

Combine the dry ingredients.

Beat together the sugar, eggs, and sour cream.

Combine the wet and dry ingredients. Add the grated chocolate.

Spoon the batter into a small greased loaf pan allowing the grated chocolate to swirl about. Be careful, if you stir too hard, you will lose the marbling effect.

Bake at 350° F. for 40 to 50 minutes.

Let the bread cool for 10 minutes before removing it from the pan.

CHERRY CHOCOLATE BREAD

This bread breaks the cake barrier. It is a dessert bread that is as close to a cake as icing. Label this "for chocolate lovers everywhere."

Dry Ingredients

3 cups unbleached flour
1 tablespoon baking powder
1 cup white sugar
½ teaspoon salt
6 ounces semi-sweet chocolate bits

Wet Ingredients

3 ounces unsweetened chocolate, melted
1 cup milk
¼ cup oil
¼ cup undyed maraschino cherry juice
½ cup drained, chopped maraschino
    cherries
1 egg, beaten

Combine the dry ingredients.

Combine the wet and dry ingredients. Spoon into a large greased loaf pan.

Bake at 350° F. for 60 to 70 minutes.

Let the bread cool for 10 minutes before removing it from the pan.

POTATO CHOCOLATE BREAD

This is an elegant bread. The potato gives it a moist-
ness and texture that is surprising. It has a definite
chocolate taste, but it is not a sweet bread.

Wet Ingredients

1 medium-size potato or
    1 cup shredded zucchini
Water
¾ cup milk
2 eggs, beaten
½ cup oil
1 ounce melted or grated unsweetened
    chocolate
½ teaspoon vanilla extract

Dry Ingredients

2½ cups unbleached flour
½ cup sugar
½ teaspoon salt
½ teaspoon baking powder
½ teaspoon baking soda

First prepare the potato. Shred the potato, cover generously with water, and cook for 5 minutes. Drain the potato. Your yield should be about one cup.

Mix together the remaining wet ingredients. Add the potato.

Combine the dry ingredients.

Mix together the dry and wet ingredients. Pour into a greased medium-size loaf pan.

Bake at 350° F. for 50 to 60 minutes.

Let the bread cool for 10 minutes before removing it from the pan.

DOUBLE CAROB BREAD

Carob isn't chocolate; chocolate lovers can't be fooled that easily. It is, however, a taste even chocolate lovers can appreciate, and it is richer in vitamins and minerals, lower in fat (about 1/10 the amount), with half the calories of chocolate. This bread is hearty and not too sweet. It is best served cold.

Dry Ingredients

1 cup light rye flour
1 cup whole wheat flour
¼ cup carob powder
½ cup carob chips
1 teaspoon baking powder
½ teaspoon salt

Wet Ingredients

2 tablespoons softened butter
⅓ cup honey
1 egg, beaten
1 cup milk

Combine the dry ingredients.

Combine the wet ingredients in a blender and mix well.

Pour the wet ingredients into the dry and stir together lightly. Spoon into a small greased loaf pan.

Bake at 350° F. for about 50 minutes.

Let the bread cool for 10 minutes before removing it from the pan.

BASIC APPLE BREAD

The challenge of baking with apple is that of preserving the apple flavor through the baking process. Applesauce and apple butter seem to work better than raw apples as a rule, but this basic apple bread will give you a hint of apple.

Dry Ingredients

2½ cups unbleached flour
½ cup sugar
2 teaspoons baking powder
½ teaspoon baking soda
½ teaspoon salt

Wet Ingredients

2 large tart apples, peeled and grated
2 eggs
¼ cup softened butter
¼ cup apple juice or cider
2 tablespoons lemon juice

Mix together the dry ingredients.

Combine the wet ingredients in a blender. Process until smooth.

Combine the wet and dry ingredients lightly. The batter will be very heavy. Spoon into a greased medium-size loaf pan.

Bake at 325° F. for 70 minutes.

Let the bread cool for 10 minutes before removing it from the pan.

Apple Butter Bread

While plain apples hint of themselves in bread, apple butter will hit you over the palate. Apple butter is produced by cooking apples until they are very thick. Cinnamon and cloves are typically added, imparting both taste and the rich brown coloring. Most commercial apple butters are heavily sweetened and so there is no need for additional sweeteners to be added to the bread.

Dry Ingredients

1½ cups unbleached flour
½ cup oat flour
½ teaspoon salt
2 teaspoons baking powder

Wet Ingredients

2 eggs
1 cup apple butter
¼ cup apple juice or cider
½ cup chopped nuts (optional)
½ cup raisins (optional)

Combine the dry ingredients.

Beat together the eggs, apple butter, and apple juice. Add the nuts and raisins.

Mix the dry and wet ingredients. Spoon the batter into a small greased loaf pan.

Bake at 350° F. for 55 minutes.

Let the bread cool for 10 minutes before removing it from the pan.

APPLE CHEDDAR BREAD

A sharp cheddar is a fine complement to a tart apple. Glenda's father used to say, "Apple pie without cheese is like a kiss without a squeeze." In this bread we combine the two to produce a moist loaf that preserves this taste combination. It makes a good dinner bread.

Dry Ingredients

2 cups unbleached flour
¼ cup sugar
½ teaspoon salt
1½ teaspoons baking powder
½ teaspoon baking soda
½ cup grated cheddar cheese

Wet Ingredients

¼ cup softened butter
2 eggs, beaten
Juice from 1 lemon
3 apples, peeled and grated (about 1 cup)

Combine the dry ingredients.

Mix together the wet ingredients.

Stir the wet and dry ingredients together until just moistened. Pour into a greased medium-size loaf pan.

Bake at 350° F. for about 1 hour.

Let the bread cool for 10 minutes before removing it from the pan.

Spiced Applesauce Bread

This is much like an applesauce cake, but better. Serve warm with butter, or cold with cream cheese. It is also a nice addition to a cheese plate. Or an empty plate.

Dry Ingredients

1 ¾ cups unbleached flour
¾ teaspoon baking soda
½ teaspoon baking powder
¼ teaspoon salt
½ teaspoon cinnamon
¼ teaspoon allspice
Grated rind of 1 lemon

Wet Ingredients

½ cup chilled butter
2 eggs, yolks separated
1 cup applesauce
½ cup chopped pecans (optional)
⅓ cup raisins (optional)

Combine the dry ingredients. Cut the butter into the flour mixture.

Mix together the egg yolks and applesauce. Combine with the dry ingredients. Add the pecans and raisins, if desired.

Whip the egg whites until stiff.

Gently fold the egg whites into the batter. Pour the batter into a greased medium-size loaf pan.

Bake at 350° F. for about 45 minutes, or until golden brown.

Let the bread cool for 10 minutes before removing it from the pan.

APPLE OAT BREAD

This may be one of the slowest quick breads we've made, but it is worth the wait. The preparation is routine, but we bake this in a slow, steamy oven. With these spices and fruits and the moist, slow baking, you have a bread that is quite close to a fruitcake.

Dry Ingredients

1¼ cups unbleached flour
¾ cup oat flour
½ teaspoon baking powder
¼ teaspoon baking soda
½ teaspoon salt
1 teaspoon cinnamon
¼ teaspoon nutmeg
½ cup raisins
½ cup chopped dates

Wet Ingredients

½ cup softened butter
½ cup brown sugar
1 cup grated tart apple
½–¾ cup buttermilk

Mix together the dry ingredients.

Cream together the butter and sugar. Add the apple and buttermilk.

Combine the wet and dry ingredients. Spoon into a greased medium-size loaf pan.

Bake at 275° F. for about 2 hours. Put a large pan of hot water in the oven to create steam while the bread is baking.

Let the bread cool for 10 minutes before removing it from the pan.

HOWARD'S APRICOT BREAD

Keep in mind three things when baking with dried apricots. First, use California dried apricots that still have their characteristic color. Second, cut the apricots into small pieces. Third, let the cut apricots sit in warmed orange juice or water for at least 30 minutes before adding to a batter.

Wet Ingredients

⅔ cup chopped dried apricots
Water
1 egg
1 cup milk
3 tablespoons oil
4 teaspoons grated orange rind

Dry Ingredients

2 cups unbleached flour
2 teaspoons baking powder
½ cup sugar
½ teaspoon salt

Put the apricots in a saucepan. Cover with water. Simmer for 15 minutes. Drain and cool. Beat together the egg, milk, oil, and orange rind. Add the cooled apricots.

Combine the dry ingredients.

Combine the wet and dry ingredients and stir just until mixed. Pour into a greased medium-size loaf pan.

Bake at 375° F. for about 1 hour.

Let the bread cool for 10 minutes before removing it from the pan.

Apricot Almond Bread

Wet Ingredients

½ cup orange juice
⅔ cup chopped dried apricots
½ cup milk
1 egg, beaten
3 tablespoons oil

Dry Ingredients

1½ cups unbleached flour
¼ cup brown rice flour
¼ cup almond meal or almond powder
½ cup sugar
½ teaspoon salt
2 teaspoons baking powder

Combine the orange juice and apricots in a saucepan. Heat gently; then let it sit for 15 to 30 minutes.

Combine the milk, egg, and oil. Add the apricots and orange juice.

Combine the dry ingredients.

Combine the wet and dry ingredients. Pour into a greased medium-size loaf pan.

Bake at 375° F. for 50 to 60 minutes.

Let the bread cool for 10 minutes before removing from the pan.

Note:

Almond powder is available at many Chinese groceries. Or you can make your own almond meal by pulverizing blanched almonds in a blender or food processor.

APRICOT ORANGE BREAD

This is a whole grain bread, contrasting the nuttiness of whole wheat with the tartness of the apricots and orange.

Wet Ingredients

⅔ cup chopped dried apricots
1 cup orange juice
1 egg
2 tablespoons oil

Dry Ingredients

2 cups unbleached flour
1 cup whole wheat flour
¼ cup white sugar
¼ cup brown sugar
2 teaspoons baking powder
¼ teaspoon baking soda
½ teaspoon salt

Combine the apricots and orange juice in a saucepan and heat gently. Let cool for about 30 minutes.

Beat together the egg and oil. Add the cooled apricots and orange juice.

Combine the dry ingredients.

Combine the wet and dry ingredients. Turn into a large greased loaf pan.

Bake at 350° F. for about 1 hour.

Let the bread cool for 10 minutes before removing from the pan.

Banana Oat Flake Bread

Banana bread is one of the best-known quick breads. Who hasn't tasted several versions of this black-flecked sweet bread? Because the banana makes the bread moist, it keeps well. This bread is best served warm.

Wet Ingredients

1 cup sliced banana
⅓ cup molasses
Juice and grated rind of 1 orange
1 egg
⅓ cup oil

Dry Ingredients

2 cups oat flake cereal
2 cups unbleached flour
2 teaspoons baking powder
¼ teaspoon salt

Combine the wet ingredients in a blender or food processor. Blend well. Stir the oat flakes into the wet ingredients and allow to soak while you prepare the remaining dry ingredients.

Combine the flour, baking powder, and salt.

Mix together all the ingredients. Pour into a greased medium-size loaf pan.

Bake at 350° F. for 60 minutes.

Let the bread cool for 10 minutes before removing from the pan.

WHOLE WHEAT BANANA BREAD

This is another not-too-sweet or overpowering banana bread.

Dry Ingredients

¾ cup unbleached flour
¾ cup whole wheat flour
1 teaspoon baking soda
½ teaspoon salt

Wet Ingredients

½ cup softened butter
½ cup sugar
1 egg, beaten
¼ cup buttermilk (or yogurt or
    sour cream)
2 medium-size bananas, mashed

Combine the dry ingredients.

Cream together the butter and sugar.

Add the egg, buttermilk, and banana. Mix well.

Combine the wet and dry ingredients. Mix just enough to combine well. Pour into a small greased loaf pan.

Bake at 350° F. for 50 to 60 minutes.

Let the bread cool for 10 minutes before removing it from the pan.

BANANA APRICOT BREAD

Even people who don't like banana bread found this an unusual treat. The apricot adds a nice tartness.

Dry Ingredients

2 cups unbleached flour
½ cup chopped almonds
⅓ cup sugar
¼ teaspoon salt
1½ teaspoons baking powder
½ teaspoon baking soda
¾ cup finely chopped dried apricots

Wet Ingredients

3 small bananas, sliced
2 eggs
⅓ cup softened butter

Combine the dry ingredients.

Mix the wet ingredients in a blender or food processor. Blend until smooth.

Combine the wet and dry ingredients. Spoon into a greased medium-size loaf pan.

Bake at 350° F. for about 1 hour.

Let the bread cool for 10 minutes before removing from the pan.

Banana Nut Bread

This makes a very crunchy bread. It keeps well if refrigerated.

Dry Ingredients

2 cups unbleached flour
½ teaspoon salt
½ teaspoon baking soda
½ cup chopped walnuts

Wet Ingredients

½ cup softened butter
½ cup brown sugar
2 eggs
1 cup sliced bananas

Combine the dry ingredients.

Combine the wet ingredients in a blender. Mix until smooth.

Combine the wet and dry ingredients. Pour into a greased medium-size loaf pan.

Bake at 350° F. for about 45 minutes.

Let the bread cool for 10 minutes before removing from the pan.

ORANGE HONEY BREAD

This is one of those quick breads that sits on the border between a cake and a bread. Sweet and rich in orange flavor, it also surprises the taste with the addition of nuts.

Dry Ingredients

2½ cups unbleached flour
2 teaspoons baking powder
½ teaspoon baking soda
½ teaspoon salt
¾ cup chopped hazelnuts or pecans

Wet Ingredients

2 tablespoons softened butter
¾ cup honey
1 egg, beaten
¾ cup orange juice
1½ tablespoons grated orange rind

Mix together the dry ingredients.

Combine the wet ingredients.

Stir the wet ingredients into the dry ingredients. Pour into a greased medium-size loaf pan.

Bake at 325° F. for about 1 hour.

Let the bread cool for 10 minutes before removing it from the pan.

THREE ORANGE BREAD

In this bread we pulled out all stops and used juice, rind, and marmalade. The result is that the orange flavor and color permeates the bread. It has a good, firm texture, and it is not too sweet to serve with a meal.

Dry Ingredients

2 cups unbleached flour
1 cup oat flour
½ cup sugar
2 teaspoons baking powder
1 teaspoon baking soda
½ teaspoon salt

Wet Ingredients

¾ cup orange juice
¼ cup orange marmalade
1 teaspoon grated orange rind
1 egg, beaten
¼ teaspoon vanilla extract

Combine the dry ingredients.

Mix together the wet ingredients.

Mix together the dry and wet ingredients. Spoon into well-greased medium-size loaf pan.

Bake at 350° for 50 minutes.

Let the bread cool for 10 minutes before removing it from the pan.

ORANGE POTATO BREAD

With the potato in this bread, you have a moist, orange, semi-sweet loaf.

Wet Ingredients

1 small potato
Water
¾ cup orange juice
¼ cup marmalade
¼ cup oil
1 egg, beaten

Dry Ingredients

3 cups unbleached flour
½ cup sugar
2 teaspoons baking powder
1 teaspoon baking soda
¼ teaspoon salt

First, shred the potato. Cook it in water to cover for about 10 minutes. Drain. Measure out ½ cup cooked shredded potato. Add the remaining wet ingredients to the potato. Mix well.

Combine the dry ingredients.

Mix together the wet and dry ingredients. Spoon into a well-greased medium-size loaf pan.

Bake at 350° F. for 50 minutes.

Let the bread cool for 10 minutes before removing it from the pan.

PEAR BREAD

In our search for new challenges, we decided to see if we could develop some tasty pear breads. Since pears have such a mild flavor, this was not an easy task. When we served this to our students, they found it exciting. Few had even conceived of a pear bread. The contrast of the deep brown crust with the white interior and almost translucent fruit made this a visually, as well as viscerally, stimulating experience. Serve this any time with softened butter.

Dry Ingredients

3 cups unbleached flour
⅓ cup nonfat dry milk
¼ cup sugar
½ teaspoon salt
1 tablespoon baking powder
4 dried pear halves, diced

Wet Ingredients

1½ cups pear nectar
1 egg
3 tablespoons oil

Combine the dry ingredients.

Beat together the wet ingredients. Mix together the wet and dry ingredients. Spoon into a large greased loaf pan.

Bake at 350° F. for about 1 hour.

Let the bread cool for 10 minutes before removing it from the pan.

TRIPLE PEAR BREAD

Dry Ingredients

2½ cups unbleached flour
4 dried pear halves, finely diced
¼ cup sugar
½ teaspoon salt
2 teaspoons baking powder
½ teaspoon ground ginger or 1-inch piece
of fresh ginger root, grated

Wet Ingredients

1 pear, peeled, cored, and sliced
¼ cup pear nectar
1 egg
1 tablespoon oil

Combine the dry ingredients.

Combine the wet ingredients in a blender or food processor. Blend until smooth.

Combine the wet and dry ingredients very lightly. Pour into a well-greased medium-size loaf pan.

Bake at 350° F. for about 1 hour. If the bread still seems as though it isn't done, turn off the oven and let it continue baking as the oven cools. This seems to be the only effective way to deal with fruit breads that don't want to get done.

Let the bread cool for 10 minutes before removing it from the pan.

PEAR, DATE, AND BRAN BREAD

Bartlett pears have such an unobtrusive taste that their flavor is almost lost in a bread with a strong flour such as bran. Pear apples, which are abundant in Chinese markets in August, or seckel pears give this bread its unique flavor.

Dry Ingredients

2 cups unbleached flour
½ cup wheat bran
¼ cup sugar
¼ teaspoon salt
2 teaspoons baking powder
¼–½ cup chopped dates

Wet Ingredients

½ cup milk
1 egg, beaten
2 tablespoons oil
2 pears, peeled and shredded
   (about 1 cup)
Grated rind of 1 lemon

Combine the dry ingredients.

Mix together the wet ingredients.

Mix together the dry and wet ingredients. Spoon into a small greased loaf pan. Let the bread sit for 20 minutes.

Bake at 350° F. for about 1 hour. When the bread is golden brown, turn off the oven and leave it in the oven to finish cooking the inside.

Let the bread cool for 10 minutes before removing it from the pan. This is excellent served cold.

COCONUT PINEAPPLE BREAD

Would any cookbook be complete without the popular piña colada taste? This is not a sweet bread and has an excellent texture. Introduced at one of our school meetings, it was a big hit with its light, subtle taste. Eat it plain. It goes well with coffee.

Dry Ingredients

3 cups unbleached flour
2 slices unsweetened dried pineapple, chopped
½ teaspoon salt
1 tablespoon baking powder
1 teaspoon grated orange rind

Wet Ingredients

1¼ cups coconut pineapple juice
1 egg, beaten
3 tablespoons oil

Combine the dry ingredients.

Mix together the wet ingredients.

Mix the dry and wet ingredients together lightly. Spoon into a large greased loaf pan.

Bake at 350° F. for about 45 minutes.

Let the bread cool for 10 minutes before removing it from the pan.

PINEAPPLE CHEESE BREAD

This is an unusual combination. The cheese makes the bread rich and smooth. Dried pineapple, which you can buy at health food stores if your grocery store doesn't stock it, gives this bread its distinctive taste. Toasting the bread renews the cheese flavor. Served with butter, Pineapple Cheese Bread goes with almost everything.

Dry Ingredients

2 ½ cups unbleached flour
2 teaspoons baking powder
½ teaspoon baking soda
¼ teaspoon salt
1 tablespoon sugar
¾ cup shredded muenster cheese

Wet Ingredients

1 cup pineapple juice
1 egg, beaten
2 tablespoons oil
½ cup chopped dried unsweetened
    pineapple

Combine the dry ingredients.

Mix together the juice, egg, and oil. Add the pineapple.

Combine the wet and dry ingredients. Spoon the batter into a greased medium-size loaf pan.

Bake at 350° F. for 45 minutes.

Let the bread cool for 10 minutes before removing it from the pan.

PINEAPPLE PRUNE BREAD

This is a rich, moist bread that is good combined with cheese or served as a breakfast or snack bread.

Dry Ingredients

2½ cups unbleached flour
2 teaspoons baking powder
½ teaspoon salt
½ cup chopped prunes
½ cup chopped dried unsweetened pineapple

Wet Ingredients

3 tablespoons honey
¼ cup milk
1 cup pineapple juice
1 egg
3 tablespoons oil

Mix together the dry ingredients.

Beat together the wet ingredients.

Combine the wet and dry ingredients. Spoon into a well-greased medium-size loaf pan.

Bake at 350° F. for 50 to 60 minutes.

Let the bread cool for 10 minutes before removing it from the pan. This is best served after it ages for a few hours.

Basic Prune Bread

Not everyone likes prunes, but even "prunophobes" can relish a prune bread. In the following recipe, we vary the flours. As you will see, the breads take on a different taste as the prune interacts with the flours.

Dry Ingredients

1 cup unbleached flour
1 cup whole wheat pastry flour
1 teaspoon baking soda
1 teaspoon baking powder
¼ teaspoon salt

Wet Ingredients

1 cup buttermilk
¼ cup malted barley syrup
2 tablespoons oil
½ cup finely diced prunes

Combine the dry ingredients.

Mix together the buttermilk, barley syrup, and oil. Add the prunes.

Combine the wet and dry ingredients. Mix gently. Spoon into a small greased loaf pan.

Bake at 350° F. for 50 to 60 minutes.

Let the bread cool for 10 minutes before removing it from the pan.

LIGHT PRUNE BREAD

In this variation of the basic prune bread we replaced the whole wheat flour with oat flour and brown rice flour. The result? A sweet nuttiness and a fine-textured, crunchy crust. This bread is outstandingly golden brown in color from the combination of ingredients.

Dry Ingredients

1¼ cups unbleached flour
½ cup oat flour
¼ cup brown rice flour
1 teaspoon baking powder
¼ teaspoon salt

Wet Ingredients

1 cup buttermilk
¼ cup malted barley syrup
2 tablespoons oil
½ cup finely diced prunes

Combine the dry ingredients.

Mix together the buttermilk, barley syrup, and oil. Add the prunes.

Combine the wet and dry ingredients. Mix gently and spoon into a small greased loaf pan.

Bake at 350° F. for 50 to 60 minutes.

Let the bread cool for 10 minutes before removing it from the pan.

PRUNE PECAN BREAD

This is a sweet, crumbly, crunchy, nutty, spiced loaf. It is distinctive in taste and texture.

Dry Ingredients

1½ cups unbleached flour
1½ cups oat flour
½ cup light brown sugar
2 teaspoons baking powder
¼ teaspoon mace
¼ teaspoon nutmeg
¼ teaspoon salt

Wet Ingredients

1⅓ cups milk
1 egg, beaten
¼ cup oil
½ cup chopped prunes
½ cup chopped pecans

Combine the dry ingredients.

Mix together the milk, egg, and oil. Add the prunes and pecans.

Combine the wet and dry ingredients. Spoon into a large greased loaf pan.

Bake at 350° F. for 50 to 60 minutes.

Let the bread cool for 10 minutes before removing it from the pan.

CHERRY BREAD

This is a rich bread that can serve as dessert, perhaps accompanied by a mild cheese. It is good warm or cold.

Dry Ingredients

2 cups unbleached flour
1 teaspoon baking soda
½ teaspoon salt

Wet Ingredients

½ cup softened butter
½ cup sugar
1 cup buttermilk
1 teaspoon vanilla extract
2 eggs, beaten
1 cup chopped pitted cherries
1 cup chopped pecans

Combine the dry ingredients.

Cream together the butter and sugar. Add the buttermilk, vanilla, eggs, cherries, and pecans.

Combine the wet and dry ingredients lightly. Spoon into a greased medium-size loaf pan. Bake at 350° F. for 55 to 60 minutes.

Let the bread cool for 10 minutes before removing it from the pan.

CRANBERRY BREAD

This is a striking bread. Not only do the bright red cranberries stand out, but their tartness embedded in this somewhat sweet dough adds still another contrast. You can prolong the cranberry season by freezing berries and defrosting them just before baking this bread.

Dry Ingredients

2 cups unbleached flour
½ cup sugar
1 tablespoon grated orange rind
½ teaspoon salt
1½ teaspoons baking powder
½ teaspoon baking soda

Wet Ingredients

¾ cup orange juice
¼ cup oil
1 cup coarsely chopped cranberries

Combine the dry ingredients.

Mix together the wet ingredients.

Mix the dry and wet ingredients lightly. This makes a thick batter. Spoon into a small greased loaf pan.

Bake at 350° F. for 50 to 60 minutes.

Let the bread cool for 10 minutes before removing it from the pan.

PURPLE PLUM BREAD

This was one of the first quick breads we ever made. The moistness of the plums calls for a longer baking time, but the bread still remains quite soft. It ages well and freezes well. Serve it with softened cream cheese for a good taste contrast.

Dry Ingredients

3 cups unbleached flour
¼ cup sugar
2 teaspoons baking powder
½ teaspoon salt
1⅓ cups chopped canned plums,
    drained well

Wet Ingredients

1 egg
¾ cup milk
½ cup orange juice
1 tablespoon grated orange rind
3 tablespoons oil

Combine the dry ingredients.

Beat together the wet ingredients.

Combine the wet and dry ingredients. Pour into a large greased loaf pan. Allow to stand for about 20 minutes.

Bake in a preheated 350° F. oven for approximately 70 minutes.

Let the bread cool for 10 minutes before removing it from the pan.

Raspberry Bread

This is a rich, decadent bread. The high fat and sugar content makes this dessert bread something you might want to serve at tea time or after a light meal.

Dry Ingredients

3 cups unbleached flour
½ teaspoon salt
¾ teaspoon cream of tartar
½ teaspoon baking soda

Wet Ingredients

½ cup softened butter
½ cup sugar
1 teaspoon rum or rum flavoring
1 tablespoon lemon juice
4 eggs
1 cup raspberry preserves
½ cup sour cream

Combine the dry ingredients.

Cream together the butter, sugar, rum or rum flavoring, and lemon juice. Beat in the eggs.

Stir together the raspberry preserves and sour cream.

Add the sour cream mixture alternately with the flour mixture to the sugar-egg mixture. Mix lightly. Spoon into a large greased loaf pan.

Bake at 350° F. for 50 to 60 minutes.

Let the bread cool for 10 minutes before removing it from the pan.

BLUEBERRY ORANGE BREAD

This was one of our very popular breads—good served hot, but even better the next day. Serve it to people who love blueberry muffins. Black raspberries make an unusual substitute for blueberries.

Dry Ingredients

3 cups unbleached flour
2 teaspoons baking powder
¼ teaspoon baking soda
½ teaspoon salt
1 cup fresh, frozen, or drained canned berries

Wet Ingredients

¼ cup honey
Grated rind and juice of 1 orange
½ cup milk
½ cup oil

Combine the dry ingredients and stir to blend thoroughly.

Beat together the wet ingredients.

Pour the wet ingredients into the dry and stir until the dry ingredients are moist. Spoon into a large well-greased loaf pan and let it stand for about 15 minutes.

Bake at 350° F. for 1 hour.

Let the bread cool for 10 minutes before removing it from the pan.

CARROT RAISIN BREAD

This is a very rich, moist bread that is great for a picnic lunch. It can even serve as dessert after a light meal.

Dry Ingredients

2 cups unbleached flour
1 teaspoon baking soda
½ teaspoon salt
½ cup raisins

Wet Ingredients

3 medium-size carrots, chopped
⅔ cup milk
½ cup softened butter
3 tablespoons honey
2 eggs

Glaze Ingredients

⅓ cup honey
**⅓ cup undiluted orange juice
   concentrate**

Mix together the dry ingredients.

Combine the wet ingredients in a blender or food processor. Process until smooth.

Combine the dry and wet ingredients. Pour into a greased 9-inch round pan.

Bake at 350° F. for 1 hour.

Let the bread cool for 10 minutes before removing it from the pan.

To make the glaze, combine the honey and orange juice concentrate and pour over the top of the bread.

The bread may be served immediately. Leftover bread should be stored in the refrigerator.

ANOTHER CARROT RAISIN BREAD

Dry Ingredients

2¼ cups unbleached flour
¾ cup whole wheat flour
2 teaspoons baking powder
½ cup candied fruit or white raisins
½ teaspoon salt
1 teaspoon cinnamon
¼ teaspoon nutmeg

Wet Ingredients

1 egg
½ cup molasses
¼ cup oil
1½ cups grated carrots
¾ cup buttermilk

Mix together the dry ingredients.

Combine the wet ingredients in a blender and process until smooth.

Mix together the wet and dry ingredients just until blended. Spoon into a large greased loaf pan.

Bake at 350° F. for 1 hour.

Let the bread cool for 10 minutes before removing it from the pan.

KUGELHUPF BREAD

This is an unusual version of a traditional holiday favorite. In its traditional form, it is made with yeast and white flour and baked in a fluted tube pan. This whole wheat adaptation will amaze you with its lightness of texture and taste.

Wet Ingredients

¼ cup softened butter
⅓ cup honey (or malted barley)
2 eggs, beaten
1 cup milk
1 teaspoon grated lemon rind
½ teaspoon vanilla extract

Dry Ingredients

2½ cups whole wheat pastry flour
1 cup golden raisins
2 teaspoons baking powder
¼ teaspoon nutmeg
½ teaspoon cinnamon
½ teaspoon salt
3 ounces sliced almonds

Beat together the wet ingredients.

Combine the dry ingredients, except the almonds.

Mix together the wet and dry ingredients.

Pour some of the sliced almonds into the bottom of a greased medium-size bread pan. Pour the batter into the pan. Sprinkle the remaining sliced almonds over the top.

Bake in a 350° F. oven for about 1 hour.

Let the bread cool for 10 minutes before removing it from the pan.

CHRISTMAS BREAD

This is a delicious bread to serve any time, but it is especially festive for the holidays. Many find this a welcome relief from the overly sweet holiday treats. The citrus flavor enhances any combination of dried fruits that you choose—apricots, prunes, pineapple, raisins, pears, peaches.

Dry Ingredients

3 cups unbleached flour
2 teaspoons baking powder
¾ teaspoon salt
⅓ cup raisins

Wet Ingredients

¼ cup honey
3 eggs
½ cup sliced banana
½ cup orange juice
½ teaspoon vanilla extract
1½ cups chopped mixed dried fruits

Mix together the dry ingredients.

Combine the honey, eggs, banana, orange juice, and vanilla in a blender. Process until smooth. Add to the dried fruits.

Combine the wet and dry ingredients, mixing well. Spoon into a large greased loaf pan.

Bake at 350° F. for about 1 hour.

Let the bread cool for 10 minutes before removing it from the pan.

STOLLEN

The Fruits

⅓ cup golden raisins
⅓ cup chopped citron
⅓ cup currants
¼ cup chopped candied orange peel
¼ cup candied lemon peel
¼ cup chopped candied pineapple
¼–½ cup cognac

Wet Ingredients

1 cup milk
1 egg, beaten
2 tablespoons oil
1½ teaspoons grated lemon peel
¼ teaspoon vanilla extract

Dry Ingredients

3 cups unbleached flour
1 tablespoon baking powder
¼ cup sugar

Combine all the fruits in a mixing bowl. Add the cognac and let the fruits soak for 1 to 2 hours.

Beat together the wet ingredients. Drain the fruits, discarding the remaining cognac, then add to the wet ingredients.

Combine the dry ingredients.

Mix together all the ingredients. This is a heavy batter, almost like a yeast bread. Knead it briefly on a lightly floured board. Shape it into an oval, about 10 inches long. With the flat edge of a knife, crease it off center lengthwise. Using your hand, roll one side of the crease until it overlaps the other. Bake at 375° F. for 40 minutes. Let the bread cool for 10 minutes before removing it from the pan.

SWEET POTATO CRANBERRY BREAD

This festive holiday bread tastes of tart cranberries and spices. It keeps well for several days; some like it better when the flavors have had a chance to blend and the cranberries are not so tart.

Dry Ingredients

2½ cups unbleached flour
½ teaspoon salt
1½ teaspoons baking powder
½ teaspoon baking soda
½ teaspoon cinnamon
¼ teaspoon nutmeg
⅓ teaspoon mace

Wet Ingredients

¾ cup cold baked sweet potato, sliced
½ cup milk
2 eggs
¼ cup softened butter
⅓ cup molasses
1 cup raw cranberries

Combine the dry ingredients.

Combine the wet ingredients in a blender or food processor and process until the cranberries are coarsely chopped.

Combine the wet and dry ingredients. Pour into a large well-greased loaf pan.

Bake at 350° F. for about 1 hour.

Let the bread cool for 10 minutes before removing it from the pan.

MINCEMEAT BREAD

Dry Ingredients

2½ cups unbleached flour
2 teaspoon baking soda

Wet Ingredients

1 (28-ounce) jar mincemeat
1⅓ cups sweetened condensed milk
2 eggs, beaten
1 ounce rum

Mix together the dry ingredients.

Combine the wet ingredients.

Mix together the dry and wet ingredients. Spoon into a greased medium-size loaf pan.

Bake at 300° F. for 1½ to 2 hours. Check the bread for firmness at the end of the first 90 minutes. Remove it from the oven when it has a firm feel and a good hollow sound.

Let the bread cool for 10 minutes before removing it from the pan.

Gingerbread

This is the most unusual gingerbread recipe we've tried. We found it in an article on beer. It works. The dark beer adds to and complements the ginger. Do use a good dark beer.

Dry Ingredients

2¼ cups unbleached flour
2 tablespoons finely chopped crystallized
    ginger
1 teaspoon cinnamon
1 teaspoon baking soda

Wet Ingredients

1 cup dark beer, at room temperature
½ cup oil
½ cup light molasses
1 egg, beaten

Combine the dry ingredients.

Mix together the wet ingredients.

Combine all ingredients, mixing well. Spoon into a greased 9-inch square baking pan.

Bake at 325° F. for 45 to 50 minutes.

Let the bread cool for 10 minutes before removing it from the pan.

SCONES AND MUFFINS

It is hard to describe a scone to someone who has never eaten one. It's lighter than a biscuit, smoother than an English muffin, heavier than a muffin, and thicker than a flat bread. Of course, you'll have to try it.

Scones come in different sizes and shapes; some are oven-baked, some cooked on a griddle or frying pan, and some are griddle-cooked and then oven-finished. They originated in Scotland, Wales, and parts of Northern England. Their variations in size—the large ones have been called bannocks in Scotland—and in ingredients seem to reflect the different regions in which they developed.

Our scones are surely modern American variations, and our basic griddle scone is made with one of Howard's favorite ingredients, sour cream.

While scones are fairly new to American kitchens, everybody knows and likes muffins. The possible variations are amazing, and you can even bake several types at the same time.

There are a few ground rules for muffin making. First, mix your batter very gently. Second, expect muffin batters to be lumpy. Third, grease your muffin cups well—including the top of the pan. Fourth, fill your muffin cups about two-thirds full. Note that all our muffin recipes are designed to fill the standard twelve-cup muffin pan. Finally, after they are baked, usually at high temperatures, let the muffins stay in the pans for about five minutes after they come out of the oven. This way you can remove them easily and keep them in one piece. Remember that muffins don't keep; they are best eaten right after baking.

GRIDDLE SCONES

Dry Ingredients

2 cups unbleached flour
2 teaspoons sugar
1 teaspoon baking soda
1 teaspoon cream of tartar
¼ teaspoon salt

Wet Ingredients

¾ cup sour cream

Combine the flour, sugar, baking soda, cream of tartar, and salt. Add the sour cream and mix briskly.

Place the dough on a floured board. Divide the dough in half and pat out each half to form a circle about ½ inch thick. The circle should be 5 to 6 inches in diameter.

Dust an ungreased griddle or frying pan with flour, add a scone, and cook over low heat. The scone will rise slightly. It will brown in 7 to 10 minutes, depending on the pan. When it is lightly browned, turn it over to brown the other side. Repeat with the second scone. Cut into quarters and serve warm.

Modern Scotch Scone

In this recipe we use "modern" flours and add currants for a taste bonus. This is a fairly sweet bread.

Dry Ingredients

1 ½ cups unbleached flour
½ cup oat flour
1 teaspoon baking soda
2 tablespoons sugar
¼ teaspoon salt

Wet Ingredients

⅓ cup butter
⅓ cup milk
¼ cup currants (or ⅓ cup dark raisins)

Mix together the dry ingredients.

Cut the butter into the dry ingredients with a pastry cutter or work it in with your fingers until the mixture resembles cornmeal. Add the milk and currants.

Knead on a lightly floured board for about 3 minutes. Shape into an 8-inch circle. Place in a lightly greased frying pan.

Bake at 375° F. for 20 to 25 minutes.

Serve warm, directly from the pan.

WHOLE WHEAT SCONES

Scones have been adapted to the growing interest in whole grains. Here's one tasty variation.

Dry Ingredients

1 cup whole wheat flour
1 cup unbleached flour
½ teaspoon baking soda
½ teaspoon cream of tartar
¼ teaspoon salt

Wet Ingredients

¾ cup buttermilk
2 tablespoons oil

Combine the dry ingredients.

Mix together the wet ingredients.

Mix together all the ingredients and knead for about 3 minutes on a floured board. Divide the dough in half and pat each half into a 5-inch or 6-inch circle about ½ inch thick.

Lightly dust an ungreased griddle or frying pan with flour, add the scone, and cook over low heat for 7 to 10 minutes. When it has lightly browned, turn to brown the other side. Serve warm.

Orange Scone

*Yellow-orange in color, moist, and thick-crumbed,
this oven-baked American scone makes a good dinner
bread. It is not sweet, but it is very orange in color.
This recipe yields one large scone.*

Dry Ingredients

2 ½ cups unbleached flour
2 tablespoons sugar
1 teaspoon baking powder
1 teaspoon baking soda
½ teaspoon salt

Wet Ingredients

¾ cup orange juice
2 tablespoons oil
1 tablespoon grated orange rind
1 egg, beaten

Mix together the dry ingredients.

Combine the wet and dry ingredients.
Spoon into a greased 8-inch round pan.

Bake at 425° F. for 15 minutes.

Serve warm, directly from the pan.

TRADITIONAL BANNOCK

In this traditional Scottish recipe, oatmeal and corn-meal are used. The bannock is first set in a greased frying pan and then finished in a medium-hot oven. The result is a hard-crusted and chewy scone.

Dry Ingredients

1 cup instant oatmeal flakes
1 cup cornmeal
1 teaspoon baking soda

Wet Ingredients

1 cup buttermilk
2 tablespoons oil
2 tablespoons honey

Mix together the dry ingredients.

Combine all the ingredients, mixing well. Spoon into a heated, greased frying pan.

Fry on low heat for about 5 minutes a side. Place the pan in a 375° F. oven and bake for 10 to 15 minutes.

Serve warm, directly from the pan.

THE 1933 MUFFIN

The best basic muffin we bake is one Howard found in a 1933 home baking book published by General Foods. The reason we call it a "basic" muffin is that you can add to it. In season, we might throw in some cranberries or blueberries. You can add mashed banana, cherries, cheddar cheese. Whatever you add, don't add more than a tablespoon to each muffin.

Dry Ingredients

2 cups unbleached flour
2 tablespoons sugar
2 teaspoons baking powder
¼ teaspoon salt

Wet Ingredients

1 cup milk
1 egg, beaten
¼ cup oil

Combine the dry ingredients.

Mix together the wet ingredients.

Stir together the dry and wet ingredients, mixing gently. Spoon into a well-greased muffin pan.

Bake at 425° F. for 25 minutes.

Let the muffins cool for 5 minutes before removing them from the pan.

Note:

If you are going to use a single filling for all the muffins, then simply add 1 cup of the filling to the batter. If you are using fruits, be sure they are well-drained. Cheese should be shredded. To add different fillings to a single batch, first spoon in the batter to fill one-third of the muffin cup. Next, add 1 heaping tablespoon of the filling. Then cover with enough batter to fill the muffin cup a bit over two-thirds full.

Bran Muffins

A popular, chewy, and firm muffin incorporates bran as a central ingredient. Bran muffins are everywhere in San Francisco. Glenda has sampled all of the "best," and recommends that you experiment with the theme by adding carrot, banana, raisin, prune, sesame seeds, nuts, or apple as your mood varies.

Dry Ingredients

1½ cups unbleached flour
1 cup bran
1 tablespoon granted orange rind
1 teaspoon baking soda
¼ teaspoon salt

Wet Ingredients

1 cup buttermilk
¼ cup light molasses
¼ cup oil

Combine the dry ingredients.

Mix together the wet ingredients.

Stir together the dry and wet ingredients. Spoon into a well-greased muffin pan.

Bake at 350° F. for 25 minutes.

Let the muffins cool for 5 minutes before removing them from the pan.

Nutty Muffins

This is one of those heavy, healthy, crunchy concoctions that will titillate your taste buds and have your diners calling for the chef.

Dry Ingredients

1½ cups whole wheat pastry flour
¼ cup soy flour
1 tablespoon baking powder
¼ teaspoon salt
1¼ cups chopped roasted unsalted
    peanuts
⅓ cup roasted unsalted sunflower seeds
¼ cup roasted sesame seeds

Wet Ingredients

1 cup milk
¼ cup oil
¼ cup malted barley syrup (or honey)
1 egg, beaten
⅓ cup currants

Mix together the dry ingredients.

Mix together the wet ingredients.

Combine the dry and wet ingredients. Mix gently and spoon into a well-greased muffin pan.

Bake at 375° F. for 15 to 20 minutes.

Let the muffins cool for 5 minutes before removing them from the pan.

OLD-FASHIONED OATMEAL MUFFINS

Brown sugar and oatmeal were probably the staples of those who began experimenting with our 1933 Muffin (see page 96). It's still good today, especially if you have any leftover cereal.

Dry Ingredients

1⅓ cups unbleached flour
2 teaspoons brown sugar
2 teaspoons baking powder
¼ teaspoon salt

Wet Ingredients

1½ cups warm milk
1 cup cooked oatmeal
2 eggs, beaten
1 tablespoon softened butter

Combine the dry ingredients.

Beat together the wet ingredients.

Combine the wet and dry ingredients. Spoon into a well-greased muffin pan.

Bake at 425° F. for 20 to 25 minutes.

Let the muffins cool for 5 minutes before removing them from the pan.

OAT MUFFINS

The sweet nuttiness of oat flour with a little brown rice flour added for the crust yields a delicious and different muffin.

Dry Ingredients

1 cup oat flour
¾ cup unbleached flour
¼ cup brown rice flour
1 tablespoon baking powder
¼ cup sugar

Wet Ingredients

1 cup milk
3 tablespoons oil
1 egg, beaten

Mix together the dry ingredients.

Mix together the wet ingredients.

Combine the dry and wet ingredients. Spoon into a well-greased muffin pan.

Bake at 425° F. for 20 minutes.

Let the muffins cool for 5 minutes before removing them from the pan.

BEER AND CHEESE MUFFINS

What could go better with a glass of beer and a slice of cheese than a beer and cheese muffin? This tangy muffin is also appropriate for serving with soups or salads.

Dry Ingredients

2 cups unbleached flour
2 tablespoons sugar
1 tablespoon baking powder
¼ teaspoon dry mustard

Wet Ingredients

1 cup beer, at room temperature
¼ cup oil
1 egg, beaten
1¼ cups (about 5 ounces) grated sharp cheddar cheese

Combine the dry ingredients.

Combine the beer, oil, and egg. Mix well. Add the cheese.

Stir together all ingredients. Spoon into a well-greased muffin pan.

Bake at 400° F. for 20 to 25 minutes.

Let the muffins cool for 5 minutes before removing them from the pan.

FINNISH BARLEY FLAT BREAD

This flat bread, known also as rieska, has a very grainy texture and the distinctive taste of barley flour. Although the ingredients are few and the preparation is simple, this is one of the great breads of the world. Serve it straight from the oven.

Dry Ingredients

2 cups barley flour
2 teaspoons sugar
2 teaspoons baking powder
¾ teaspoon salt

Wet Ingredients

1 cup light cream
2 tablespoons oil

Combine the dry ingredients.

Combine the wet ingredients.

Combine the dry and wet ingredients, mixing quickly. Spoon onto a greased 15-inch baking sheet or a 12-inch pizza pan.

Pat the dough into a circle with an approximate diameter of 12 inches. The dough will not be more than ½ inch thick. Prick all over with a fork.

Bake at 450° F. for 10 minutes.

Cut into wedges. Serve warm, directly from the oven.

QUICK ONION FLAT BREAD

Dry Ingredients

1⅓ cups unbleached flour
¼ teaspoon salt
2 teaspoons baking powder

Wet Ingredients

¼ cup plus 2 tablespoons water
2½ tablespoons oil

Topping Ingredients

2 tablespoons butter
¼ cup minced onion
1 egg, beaten
1 tablespoon water
1 teaspoon poppy seeds
1 teaspoon sesame seeds

Mix together the dry ingredients.

Mix together the wet ingredients.

Combine the wet and dry ingredients. Knead the bread gently on a lightly floured board for about 1 minute. Pat it out to a thickness of about ½ inch onto a greased 12-inch pizza pan.

Melt the butter in a frying pan over low heat. Add the onions and fry gently over low heat until golden.

Brush the top of the bread with a beaten egg to which you have added 1 tablespoon of water. Distribute the onions over the bread, then sprinkle with the poppy seeds and sesame seeds.

Bake at 500° F. for 8 to 10 minutes. Serve warm, directly from the oven.

Sunflower Barley Flat Bread

Dry Ingredients

1½ cups barley flour
¼ cup unbleached flour
¼ cup sunflower meal
1 tablespoon sugar
¾ teaspoon salt
1 tablespoon baking powder

Wet Ingredients

1 cup milk
2 tablespoons oil

Mix together the dry ingredients.

Combine the wet ingredients.

Stir together the wet and dry ingredients. Spoon the batter onto a well-greased 15-inch baking sheet. Pat the dough into a 12-inch circle about ½ inch thick. Prick all over with a fork.

Bake at 450° F. for 10 minutes. Serve warm, directly from the oven.

Note:

Barley flour and sunflower seeds are both available in health food stores. To make sunflower meal, pulverize ½ cup of roasted unsalted sunflower seeds in a blender or food processor. Measure out the amount needed.

CHAPPATIS

Indian cookery has an extraordinary variety of quick flat breads. Often they are fried in clarified butter, though many are baked.

1½ cups whole wheat flour
½ cup water

Mix together the flour and water. Knead in the mixing bowl for a few minutes. Cover with a damp towel and let it rest for about 20 minutes.

Form the dough into about 8 balls. Clap each ball in your hands until somewhat flattened. Place on a floured surface and flatten until a very thin 6-inch circle is formed.

Bake on a heated, ungreased skillet for a few minutes. Turn when the surface begins to bubble. Brown the other side. They will be lightly puffed when done. Serve hot.

COCONUT CHAPPATIS

½ cup unbleached flour
⅓ cup unsweetened shredded coconut
¼ teaspoon salt
Pinch of white or cayenne pepper
3–5 tablespoons water

Mix the flour, coconut, salt, and pepper. Work in the water to make a firm dough.

Divide the dough into 6 parts. On a well-floured board, roll each piece into a small circle about 3 inches in diameter.

Cook the breads in a generously buttered frying pan until they are lightly browned on both sides.

To keep warm until ready to serve, cover with a towel and place them in a 250° F. oven.

POORIS

This is an Indian fried bread that is traditionally served with curries.

4 cups whole wheat flour
1 teaspoon salt
¼ cup ghee (clarified butter) or oil
2 cups yogurt

Combine all the ingredients. Knead the dough on a floured surface until it has a good spring to it. Cover the bowl and let stand at room temperature for about 30 minutes.

On a lightly floured surface, roll out the dough very thin. Cut into saucer-size pancakes about 6 inches in diameter. Fry in ½ inch of very hot clarified butter or oil until the poori is a light brown color. Drain on paper, and continue until all are cooked.

Pooris may be served hot or cold. To keep them warm while the full batch is fried, place them on paper towels in a baking dish in a 250° F. oven.

A Basic Cracker

Dry Ingredients

2 cups unbleached flour
½ teaspoon salt
½ teaspoon baking powder

Wet Ingredients

¼ cup chilled butter
½ cup milk
1 egg, beaten

Mix together the dry ingredients.

Cut the butter into the flour mixture with a pastry cutter or work it in with your fingers until the mixture is mealy in appearance. Add the milk and egg.

Knead thoroughly on a lightly floured surface until the dough has a good spring to it. Then roll the dough out very thin. Cut into squares or rounds and place on greased baking sheets. Prick the crackers with a fork. Expect 4 to 5 dozen standard-size crackers.

Bake in 400° F. oven for 10 minutes.

Remove from the oven and, using a spatula, place the crackers on wire racks to cool.

Rye Crackers

Dry Ingredients

1 cup rye flour
1 cup unbleached flour
½ teaspoon salt

Wet Ingredients

½ cup milk
½ cup melted butter

Combine the dry ingredients.

Mix together the wet ingredients.

Mix together all the ingredients and knead until the dough develops a light springiness. On a lightly floured board, roll the dough into ropes with a diameter of about 1 inch. Cut off thin slices and roll each slice so you have about a 3-inch cracker. You should get close to 4 dozen crackers. Place on lightly greased baking sheets.

Bake at 400° F. for 10 minutes or until lightly browned.

Remove the crackers from the sheets and cool on wire racks.

GRAHAM CRACKERS

This cracker was named after Dr. Graham, a mid-nineteenth century nutritionist who advocated eating whole wheat rather than white flour.

Dry Ingredients

2 cups whole wheat pastry or graham flour
½ teaspoon salt
1 teaspoon baking soda

Wet Ingredients

¼ cup honey
½ cup sour cream

Combine the dry ingredients. Stir in the wet ingredients.

Knead gently in the mixing bowl for about 2 minutes. On a floured board, roll out the dough to about ¼ inch thick.

Cut into whatever cracker size you prefer, then gently transfer with a spatula to 15-inch greased baking sheets.

Bake in a 375° F. oven for about 10 minutes.

Remove the crackers from the sheets and cool on wire racks.

WHOLE WHEAT OAT CRACKERS

Sometimes called a hardtack, this is a crisp, rough-textured cracker.

Dry Ingredients

1¾ cups whole wheat flour
1 tablespoon sesame seeds
1 cup quick-cooking oats
½ teaspoon baking soda

Wet Ingredients

¼ cup unsalted softened margarine
¾ cup buttermilk

Combine the dry ingredients, reserving ¼ cup of the oats. Cream together the margarine and dry ingredients. Add the buttermilk. Mix lightly. Divide the dough in half, and flatten each half to form a square about 7 inches across. Refrigerate until the dough is firm.

When ready, roll out the dough on a well-floured surface. Each half should fill a standard large 14–inch by 17–inch baking sheet. Oil the baking sheets, then sprinkle with the remaining oats. Put the dough on the sheets and pat it out to fill the space. Prick the dough all over with a fork. Then cut into cracker sizes (a pastry wheel or pizza cutter will do a good job).

Bake at 325° F. for 15 to 20 minutes. The crackers should be golden brown and crisp. Remove crackers to wire racks and allow them to cool thoroughly.

POTATO CRACKERS

1 cup mashed potatoes
1½ cups unbleached flour (more if the
  potatoes are moist, less if they are dry)
½ cup butter, melted

Mix all the ingredients together to form a stiff dough ball. Divide the dough into fourths and roll out each portion on a well-floured board. Try to get the dough thinner than ⅛ of an inch. Gently place the dough on greased baking sheets.

Bake at 375° F. for 10 to 12 minutes. The crackers are done when they begin to brown. While still soft, cut into whatever size crackers you prefer and place on a cooling rack.

Specialty Cookbooks from The Crossing Press

Biscotti, Brownies, and Bars

By Terri Henry

This collection of easy-to-follow recipes presents more than 70 recipes for cookies baked in a pan.

$6.95 • Paper • ISBN 0-89594-901-6

Old World Breads

By Charel Scheele

In this book, the art of old world bread-making is available to everyone. Instructions are given to get brick oven results from an ordinary oven using a simple clay flower-pot saucer.

$6.95 • Paper • ISBN 0-89594-902-4

Pestos! Cooking with Herb Pastes

By Dorothy Rankin

"An inventive and tasteful collection—it makes the possibilities of herb pastes enticing."

—*Publishers Weekly*

$8.95 • Paper • ISBN 0-89594-180-5

Sauces for Pasta!

By K. Trabant with A. Chesman

"This little book has my favorite new and old sauces."

—Grace Kirschenbaum, *World of Cookbooks*

$8.95 • Paper • ISBN 0-89594-403-0

Salad Dressings

By Teresa H. Burns

Making fresh salad dressings is easy! This handy little book is full of creative dressings that are fresh, healthy, and delicious.

$6.95 • Paper • ISBN 0-89594-895-8

Salsas!

By Andrea Chesman

"Appeals to me because of the recipes' originality and far-ranging usefulness."

—Elliot Mackle, *Creative Loafing*

$8.95 • Paper • ISBN 0-89594-178-3

Sun-Dried Tomatoes

By Andrea Chesman

Chesman's simple recipes include a savory selection of appetizers, salads, pastas, and breads as well as instructions for drying tomatoes at home.

$6.95 • Paper • ISBN 0-89594-900-8

To receive a catalog from The Crossing Press, please call toll-free, 800-777-1048.
Visit our Website on the Internet at:
www.crossingpress.com